Scout the Lookout

by Abbie Rushton

illustrated by Ella Hobbis

This is Scout. He is part of a mob.
A mob is a team.

The team sleeps in a heap in a burrow.

Each day, the team needs a lookout. The lookout checks for predators. It is an important job.

It is Scout's dream to be the lookout.

One day, his dream comes true …

Scout stands high on a mound.

The team hunts for grubs. Scout looks all around.

Just then, Scout spots an adder! He cries out to alert his team.

The team stand up on their paws.
They hiss and fluff up their fur.

The adder slithers off.

However, Scout has missed something.
A hawk.

Scout looks round. He sees the bird!
Then he shouts as loud as he can.

The team kick and dig with their claws. They stir up a swirling cloud of dust.

The hawk cannot see the team under the dust. They dash to the burrow.

The team is all right!

Scout twirls around. He is filled with joy.

Just then, the hawk swoops down.

Look out, Scout! Scout darts off.

Scout dashes for the burrow. The hawk pursues him.

Quick, Scout! Run!

The hawk screeches. It flies down.
It is about to grab Scout!

Scout is near the burrow.

"Come on, Scout!" shouts the team.

All of a sudden, a jackal appears!

The hawk looks round in shock.

Scout bounds off.

Scout skids into the burrow.

"Not today, hawk!" he says.

The team cries out with joy.

Scout peeps out. The hawk is attacking the jackal!

The jackal's jaws snap.

The hawk's claws grab.

The hawk flies off. Then the jackal trots away. The team can go back out.

Scout feels dismayed. He did his best, but he was not a good lookout.

“You were a *top* lookout, Scout!” cries the team.

Scout stands on his mound and feels proud!

The Lookout

Top facts about the lookout.

The lookout gets to the highest spot to look around. This might be a mound or a tree.

The lookout has different alarm cries. They tell the team what sort of predator is about.

The lookout checks if it is safe for the team to come out of the burrow again.

Encourage students to talk about the facts they have just read. Do they find any of them surprising?